"The Bible is filled with mystery, paradox, and surprise after surprise.
Who can communicate this deep reality to children better than the inimitable and uniquely gifted Randall Goodgame? Children will love this book, and their parents will too. In reading this together, the whole family will be brought back again and again to the biggest surprise of all: the good news of Jesus the Servant-King."

RUSSELL MOORE, Author, *Onward* and *The Storm-Tossed Family*

"This lovely and fun little picture book packs a big punch of powerful significance.
I want to go back in time and read this to myself as a child. I want my kids and the children in my life to know this by heart. Like Randall Goodgame's fantastic music, this book somehow harmonizes faithfulness with fun. It's enjoyable as a story, but the message of the book is a truthful, generous gift to kids desperate for clarity on who Jesus is. The good news is that the good news is good news. And Randall Goodgame is all about bringing it to kids. This book might be his best gift yet."

S.D. SMITH, Author, *The Green Ember* Series

"'The moral of the story is...' can devolve into an insufficient story ending, even though it is a very popular one. If the main message we are giving our kids is that they need to try harder, achieve more, and serve better, we are missing our opportunity to introduce them to the source of all that is good, including all that is good in them— Jesus. Randall does a lovely job of letting us know that our future is bright because Jesus has already done all the work to get us home, and he does it in a way that is accessible to kids from one to ninety-two."

SCOTT SAULS, Senior Pastor, Christ Presbyterian Church, Nashville;
Author, *Jesus Outside the Lines* and *Irresistible Faith*

"It is a rare and wonderful thing to find someone so immensely talented who submits that talent to Jesus by sharing the gospel with children. For years, Randall has been looking young people in the eye and telling them—through song and story and good humor—the astonishing truth of the gospel. It's no surprise that Randall's book about surprises does that very thing."

ANDREW PETERSON, Musician; Author

Jesus and the Very Big Surprise
© Randall Goodgame / Catalina Echeverri 2020. Reprinted 2021 (twice), 2022.

Illustrated by Catalina Echeverri | Design & Art Direction by André Parker

"The Good Book For Children" is an imprint of The Good Book Company Ltd
North America: www.thegoodbook.com UK: www.thegoodbook.co.uk
Australia: www.thegoodbook.com.au New Zealand: www.thegoodbook.co.nz
India: www.thegoodbook.co.in

ISBN: 9781784984410 | Printed in India

thegoodbook
for children

JESUS
and the
VERY
BIG
SURPRISE

RANDALL
GOODGAME

CATALINA
ECHEVERYI

Jesus
always
surprises
everybody.

Even
though
he is the
Maker of
all the
planets and
galaxies
in the
UNIVERSE...

SURPRISE!

He came to earth as
a little baby.

And even though
he is the

KING
OF
KINGS

he wasn't born in a big, beautiful palace. Instead...

SURPRISE!

He was born in a little stable
where the smelly animals lived.

When Jesus grew up and started preaching and teaching, he surprised people all the time.

One of his very favorite ways to surprise people was by telling them stories about what God is really like.

Some people thought God was always angry. Some people thought God was a trickster who liked to make bad things happen.

And some people thought God didn't care about them at all.

Of course, Jesus knew exactly what God was like. So he told a story about God's love in a way that would surprise EVERYBODY...
even you.

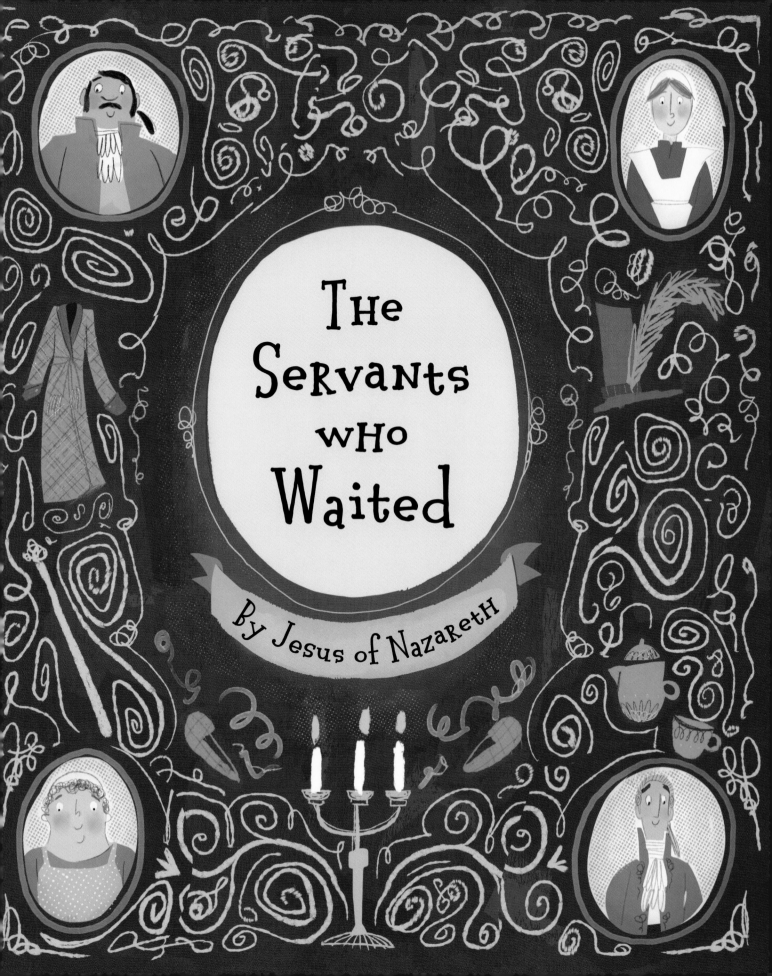

The Servants who Waited

By Jesus of Nazareth

with candles burning bright.

The servants had to be ready for

Jesus told a story about servants
waiting for their big fancy master to
come home from a great big wedding.

It was their job to watch and wait,

the moment the master would return.

But that isn't easy! When the master is away, the servants keep very busy.

There are dishes to wash,

and animals to feed,

and clothes to clean,

and pipe
organs to
polish!

And when all *that* work is done, the servants *still* need to be ready. When the master comes home, they will...

serve him a midnight snack,

fluff his pillow,

bring him his best robe,

and read
him a
bedtime
story.

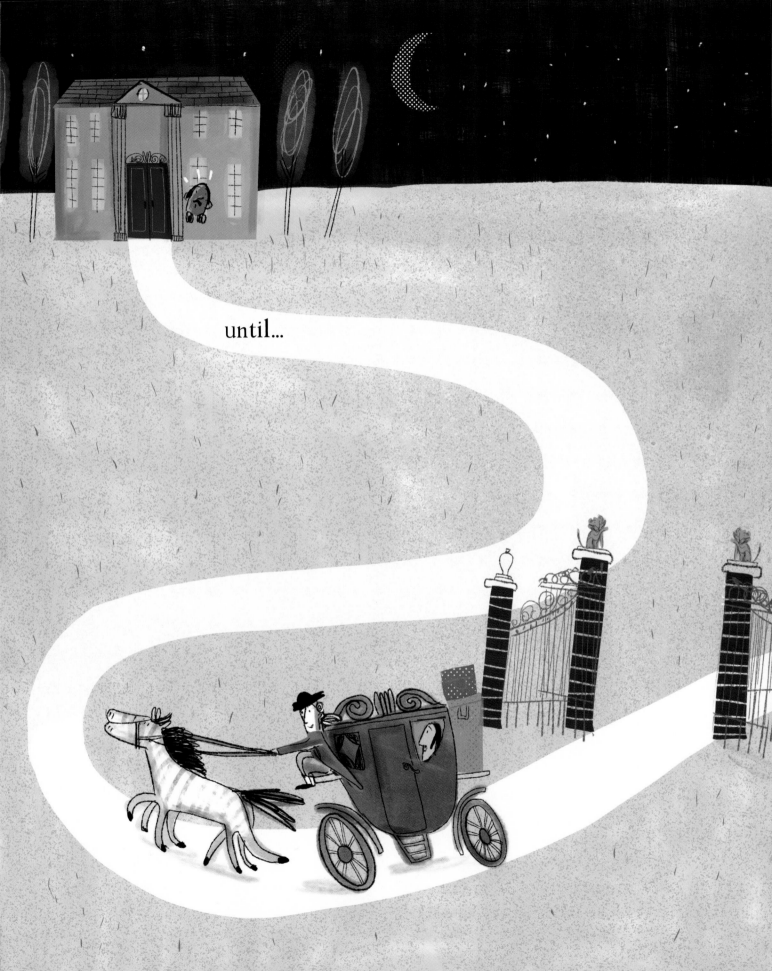

until...

Finally!

The master returns. But
the servants are in for
a big...

"Come and rest!" says the master.
"You must be tired from waiting up for me.

"Come and sit down at my table,
and I will serve you! I Know
just what you need!"

The End

In Jesus' story, the master loves his servants so much that he puts on servants' clothes, and *he* serves *them* instead!

What kind of master would love like that? What kind of God would choose to be a servant?

SURPRISE!

Jesus would.

He is the Great Master
who serves.
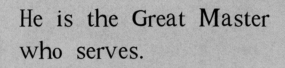

Like the master in the story, Jesus surprised everyone by using his power to serve.

He suffered...

But Jesus still
had one more
very big...

... and died on the
cross so we could live
with him forever.

SURPRISE!

He came alive again!

Then he went back to his
Father in heaven, and sent
his Holy Spirit to stay with
us till he returns.

No one knows the day or hour when Jesus will return (it could be any minute!).

And just like the servants in his story, we have plenty to do while we wait!

There are hungry people to serve,

lonely people to care for,

friends to share with,

and enemies to forgive.

And it all begins with loving Jesus, the Great Master who serves.

He knows what we need,
because he IS what we need.

So get ready —

the Master is coming!

HOW DO WE KNOW ABOUT
JESUS' RETURN?

The story, or "parable," that Jesus told about the master and his servants, and what Jesus told his disciples about how to wait for him to come back, was written down for us by Luke (who had met and interviewed a lot of the people who knew Jesus) in the New Testament part of the Bible. You'll find it in Luke 12 v 35-38. Jesus wanted his disciples—and us—to "be ready," because he "is coming at an hour you do not expect" (v 40, ESV).

Jesus spoke a lot about his return—what it would be like and how to wait for it. Here are a few other passages which give us more details: Luke 13 v 24-30; 17 v 22-35; 19 v 11-27; Matthew 25 v 1-13, 31-46.

This little story in Luke 12 is a wonderful one to memorize—I wrote a song using its words to help with that. It's called "Be Dressed," and it's Track 7 on the album Sing the Bible Volume 1. Enjoy!

Tales that Tell the Truth

Enjoy all of the award-winning "Tales That Tell The Truth" series: